More Praise for
ALL FOR THE MASTER

Many have been privileged to hear Dan Celia's devotional messages on the radio, but now everyone has the opportunity to benefit from Dan's biblical admonitions on stewardship in written form. Highlighting numerous principles related to the use of money, talents, and God's blessings, Dan focuses our attention on the eternal debt we owe to God and asks the reader to consider this central question and theme: *In what way can I best serve my Master with what He has given me and placed under my management?* If you're a serious Christ-follower who wonders why the Bible speaks more often about stewardship than it does about salvation, then you'll appreciate the insights Dan shares from his heart in this book.

—Robert W. Sayer,
U.S. Director,
Arab World Ministries

Dan Celia strikes at our hearts. It's God's Word confronting us with our responsibilities as beneficiaries of His grace. Vital to every Christian who is serious about applying stewardship principles to day-to-day living—financial decisions and so much more!

—William E. Sutter,
Executive Director,
The Friends of Israel

T0321529

In the materialistic world of our day, far too few Christians are able to think and act beyond caring for their own needs and desires as well as those of their family. Dan offers a reorientation of priorities for followers of Jesus Christ that encourages them not to shrink from God's greater blessings for them but to invest in the broader Christian global mission.

W. Sherrill Babb,
President,
Philadelphia Biblical University

ALL
FOR THE
MASTER

Reflections on the Stewardship of Our Gifts

Daniel J. Celia

All Scripture quotations, unless otherwise indicated, are taken from the New King James Version®. Copyright © 1979, 1980, 1982 by Thomas Nelson, Inc. Used by permission. All rights reserved.

Scripture marked NIV have been taken from the Holy Bible, *New International Version*, copyright © 1973, 1978, 1984 by International Bible Society. Used by permission of Zondervan. All rights reserved.

Printed in the United States of America
1 2 3 4 5—10 09 08 07 06

ISBN 978-0-7852-8969-2

DEDICATED TO

PHILADELPHIA BIBLICAL UNIVERSITY
and
to all of those ministries dependent upon each dollar
for their proclamation of the gospel.

In Appreciation Of

Philadelphia Biblical University
for their mission and ministry of graduating students
who can stand firmly on and carry the gospel
into the world that so desperately needs it. For an
educational climate that not only fosters the develop-
ment of intellectual and spiritual maturity but educates
our future leaders who possess a foundational knowledge of the Scriptures and a biblical world view.
I thank the administrative staff, faculty, and especially,

Dr. W. Sherrill Babb
for his encouragement through this project and allowing
me to participate in the ministry of PBU and
The Regency Foundation.

My administrative assistant, Pat O'Toole
For her time, work, and commitment.

To my wife and two daughters
Your walk is inspirational; your love is incredible.
Thank you for your encouragement.

To Dr. Lynette Menefee
For your insights and your labor of love for the
Kingdom. Your work and help with this book is immea-
surably appreciated.

CONTENTS

FOREWORD

Numerous books have been published on the topic of money and Christian stewardship. They generally talk about money: how to earn it, invest it, and give it for God's work. Some of these provide helpful suggestions and insights. However, there is much more that can and should be said about the ownership of God and His Son Jesus Christ over all that Christians possess and the way they are to relate these resources to their Lord.

Dan leads the reader through a 40-day adventure on key issues relating to Christians and their relationship and commitment to God. It is in this context that believers discover biblical answers to questions about the partnership they have with God and His plan for reaching the world with the gospel of Jesus Christ. Ultimately, Christians should conclude that all they are and have is "for the Master."

In the materialistic world of our day, far too few Christians are able to think and act beyond caring for their own needs and desires as well as those of their family. Dan offers a reorientation of priorities for followers of Jesus Christ that encourages them not to shrink from God's greater blessings for them but to invest in the broader Christian global mission.

Dr. W. Sherrill Babb
President
Philadelphia Biblical University
Langhorne, Pennsylvania

PREFACE

When William Carey, the great servant of the Lord and missionary to India, was a young man traveling about the hamlets and villages of England preaching the gospel, he was told, "Carey, while you are about doing this work, you are neglecting your business." Carey replied, "This is my business. I only cobble shoes to pay the expenses." We can learn so much from that simple statement. What an awesome testimony, not only to the talents and gifts God has given us—such as the gift to earn a living to provide for our families—but also to an understanding that these gifts (our talents, our time, and our abilities, as well as the resources we may gain from using these gifts) are the Lord's.

As you go through these daily devotionals, my prayer is that you would contemplate them with an open mind and an open heart, and begin to understand that everything we are, everything we do, and everything we have are gifts from God. I believe that when we truly begin to understand the ownership of all things, our relationship with our Lord and Savior will be taken to a whole different level of fellowship. As you surrender everything to the Lord, He will provide you with a deep sense of joy from serving Him.

One of my favorite Bible verses is 2 Timothy 4:7. Think about this verse as you read. Paul has an opportunity to sum up his life of more than 30 years as a missionary and one of the greatest theologians and evangelists ever to walk the earth. Paul could have been inspired to write many things to Timothy as he drew conclusions about his life. In a very short verse, using athletic-type analogies as he often does in his epistles, Paul says, "I have fought the good fight. I have finished the race. I have kept the faith." He then draws a picture for us of a faithful steward of the gospel of Jesus Christ. Paul reminds Timothy, as he reminds us today, that of all his accomplishments, the greatest thing he did in his walk of faith was to be a steward of the gospel of the Lord Jesus Christ.

We have been called first to be stewards of the gospel. That stewardship should be the foundation upon which we stand for all of our needs: our resources, time, talents, gifts, and money.

As we begin to understand the responsibility God has entrusted to us—the stewardship of the gospel—we should also understand that one of the greatest gifts we possess (one of the best ways we may have to be a steward of the gospel) may come to us through an awesome act of worship—the act of giving back to the Lord so the kingdom of Christ will grow.

My prayer is that these devotionals will help you to build a solid foundation and give you an understanding of the ownership of all with which the Lord has blessed you. If part of your worship is to give even one dollar from your heart or one day's service to the Lord's work, then I thank you from the bottom of my heart, as I remind you of what the Lord told Moses, "speak to the children of Israel, that they bring me an offering. From everyone who gives it willingly with his heart..." (Ex 25:2). Let us give as our heart would lead. I pray God's words about stewardship in this book will touch your heart and lead you to greater acts of service for His Kingdom.

ALL
FOR THE
MASTER

Reflections on the
Stewardship of Our Gifts

DAY 1

PSALM 69:30
I will praise the name of God
with a song,
And will magnify Him
with thanksgiving.

LUKE 2:20
Then the shepherds returned,
glorifying and praising God
for all the things that
they had heard and seen,
as it was told unto them.

RESPOND TO HIS GLORY

Peter tells us in 1 Peter 5:11, *To Him be the glory and the dominion forever and ever. Amen.* I love this verse. *To Him be the glory"* And...*forever and ever...* If we want to walk in the glory and the grace of God forever, then one of the things I believe Peter is telling us is that we should be in perpetual recognition of God's glory and Lordship. If we constantly recognize all that God has given us, then the Lord is going to take great joy in giving to us—the ones who are His good and faithful servants. Our future becomes pretty predictable, exciting, and awesome when we think that biblical stewardship is about recognizing and responding to His Lordship. Stop for a minute and imagine how what you do each day might be different if you truly responded to God's glory. If you keep His glory in front of your heart at all times, it will be difficult to be anything but a good steward of the resources God has given you. Our stewardship is a response to His glory and Lordship. Continue to respond to God by giving back to Him, then sit back and see how God will continue to respond and pour out His blessings upon you.

DAY 2

ROMANS 15:16-17

That I might be a minister of
Jesus Christ to the Gentiles,
ministering the gospel of God,
that the offering of the Gentiles
might be acceptable,
sanctified by the Holy Spirit.
Therefore I have reason to
glory in Christ Jesus
in the things *which pertain* to God.

PHILIPPIANS 1:27

Only let your conduct be worthy
of the gospel of Christ,
so that whether I come and see
you or am absent,
I may hear of your affairs,
that you stand fast in one spirit,
with one mind striving together
for the faith of the gospel.

GRACE OF GOD

Paul tells us in 1 Corinthians 4:1-2, *Let a man so consider us, as servants of Christ and stewards of the mysteries of God. Moreover it is required in stewards that one be found faithful.* Do we understand that our stewardship, as believers, is more than giving financially to Kingdom work? I don't believe that a full requirement of us as stewards can be met by just giving money. We must first start with the foundation, which is the stewardship of the gospel. Each of us—every believer—is a steward of the grace of God. What a scary thing—think about it! Because I have placed my faith in Jesus, because I am a believer, Paul tells me that I am a steward of the gospel. I don't know if I *want* to be a steward of the gospel. That is an awesome responsibility.

But how do we do that? We can't all be preachers and teachers, missionaries and pastors, or theologians; yet all of us are called to be stewards of the gospel. I believe that stewardship of the gospel is the foundation. It is the very beginning. It is everything that our future is built upon. If we are going to walk in the light of God, if we are going to expect His faithfulness upon our life today and upon our future, we need to be faithful stewards of the gospel of Jesus Christ. Although I may not be a missionary, I can give to missionaries. Although I may not be a pastor of our church, I can give to my church with my time and service as well as my finances. As long as my church is proclaiming the gospel, I want to keep it financially healthy so that proclamation can continue. Although we may not all be theologians or teachers, we can support those organizations or universities that are proclaiming the gospel and teaching biblical worldviews.

It is amazing how God will use the resources He has given us so we might be able to be stewards of the gospel using those resources. As we have received the grace of God, let's use our resources to participate in proclaiming the grace of God.

Day 3

LUKE 10:2
Then He said to them,
"The harvest truly *is* great,
but the laborers *are* few;
therefore pray the Lord of the harvest
to send out laborers into His harvest."

ROMANS 15:8-9
Now I say that Jesus Christ has become
a servant to the circumcision
for the truth of God, to confirm the promises
made to the fathers,
and that the Gentiles might glorify God for
His mercy, as it is written:
"For this reason I will confess to
you among the Gentiles,
and sing to Your name."

WORK YET TO BE DONE

Someone gave me a quote that we would be well served to think about. It was from a fellow named Andrew Murray, who lived more than a hundred years ago. It goes like this: "What a wonderful religion Christianity is. It takes money—the very embodiment of power of this world, with its self-interest, its covetousness, its pride, and it changes it to an instrument for God's service and glory." What a great quote! Money certainly is the embodiment of power in this world, but the power of the next world, our eternal life, is what should drive us to service and giving for the glory of God. If we are ever going to enjoy God's plan for our future—if we are going to experience the greatness that God has in His heart for us—we must always be working for the power, glory, and prosperity of the eternal world, not for the power of the present world.

I love to see how God can turn money into such a powerful instrument of His love and glory. Have you seen it, too? We just have to be willing to participate. In our giving, our stewardship, and our recognition of all that God has done for us, we are mindful that there is still much work to be done. We need to keep in mind the magnitude and glory of the work to be done for Jesus Christ. Ask the Lord today to make you mindful of His plan for you to help with the work yet to be done.

Day 4

Romans 15:15-17

Nevertheless, brethren, I have written more
boldly to you on *some* points,
as reminding you, because of the grace
given to me by God,
that I might be a minister of Jesus Christ
to the Gentiles,
ministering the gospel of God,
that the offering of the Gentiles
might be acceptable,
sanctified by the Holy Spirit.
Therefore I have reason to glory in Christ Jesus
in the things *which pertain* to God.

2 Timothy 3:15-17 (NIV)

And how from infancy you have known
the holy Scriptures,
which are able to make you wise for salvation
through faith in Christ Jesus.
All Scripture is God-breathed and
is useful for teaching,
rebuking, correcting and training
in righteousness,
so that the man of God may be thoroughly
equipped for every good work.

THE BEAUTY OF MONEY

Money certainly should not be considered a supreme necessity when it comes to ministry, but it is usually an important necessity. In every ministry and church, programs expand and contract with the income. Money means the ability to provide Christian services and ministry—to preach the gospel, provide religious education, and spread the good news of Christ.

Money can certainly be a beautiful thing when it comes to expanding the Kingdom of Christ. We ought to value and spend it for what it will do in the lives of others. My children, from the day they earned their first babysitting dollar, understood the importance of tithing. At the prodding of their mother and me, they would always set aside 10 percent of everything they earned. Now that they are grown, I know tithing is a part of their worship—it is habit as adults. I no longer have to ask them if they are tithing their earnings. It is second nature. They understand that through their giving, they get to preach the gospel and expand the Kingdom of Christ. Money can be a beautiful thing in the hands of faithful and well-equipped Christians.

DAY 5

PSALM 39:6-7

Surely every man walks about like a shadow;
Surely they busy themselves in vain;
He heaps up *riches*,
and does not know who will gather them.
"And now, Lord, what do I wait for?
My hope *is* in you."

MATTHEW 6:20-21

But lay up for yourselves treasures
in heaven,
where neither moth nor rust destroys
and where thieves do not break in and steal.
For where your treasure is,
there your heart will be also.

Where Is Our Treasure?

Jesus tells us in Matthew 6:21: *For where your treasure is, there your heart will be also.* The great preacher, Henry Ward Beecher, once said, "No man can tell whether he is rich or poor by turning to his ledger. It is the heart that makes a man rich. He is rich according to *what he is,* not according to *what he has*" (emphasis mine).

What we feel in our hearts helps reveal God's will for us. It is our hearts that will clearly help us to understand the stewardship of our possessions. Everybody's definition of being rich or having prosperity is different. I know I feel incredibly rich as a man and a husband and a father. But if I said that to a man who was exceptionally rich monetarily, he would probably think I was crazy.

The joy we take in our future and our prosperity is certainly known to God, and I believe sometimes we already possess it in our hearts. Sometimes God grows our wealth and prosperity by growing our ability to walk closer with Him. I have been blessed with the opportunity to speak with many people, and I love to speak with people who have spent the majority of their lives on the mission field. They have seen God's hand at work much more than you or I have. They have an incredible appreciation for true wealth, so much so that their monetary value seems almost meaningless. Their treasure is truly in their hearts. We all need to pray that our hearts can be made truly wealthy and full of real treasure.

Day 6

Matthew 13:24
Another parable He put forth to them, saying:
"The kingdom of heaven is like a man who
sowed good seed in his field.

Matthew 13:37-39
He answered and said to them:
"He who sows the good seed
is the Son of Man.
The field is the world, the good seeds
are the sons of the kingdom,
but the tares are the sons of the wicked *one*.
The enemy who sowed them is the devil,
the harvest is the end of the age,
and the reapers are the angels."

SCATTER AND SOW

Look at Proverbs 11:24: *There is one who scatters, yet increases more; And there is one who withholds more than is right, But it leads to poverty.* It's amazing to me how many of us believe that, if we save and save that someday, we will have riches. I believe God's Word is pretty clear that, though we may hold back, we may not necessarily see our wealth increase. It's those who scatter and sow who will reap a harvest. Now some of us may fail in our stewardship because of our hoarding. However, there are a number of people who, unfortunately, fail because of their spending. It is the sowing of the seed for God-honoring purposes that will bring us riches and true wealth.

I guess the question you have to ask yourself is whether you are okay with receiving true wealth. As we sit back and analyze our hearts, are we looking for true wealth or worldly wealth? Are we looking for the recognition of our neighbors and friends and wealth as it is perceived by the world? Listen, God has a great plan for you. God wants you to prosper and He will prosper you. Think about your definition of prosperity. Would it be Webster's definition or would it be the biblical definition?

DAY 7

PSALM 39:6-7

Surely every man walks about like a shadow;
Surely they busy themselves in vain;
He heaps up *riches*,
And does not know who will gather them.
"And now, Lord, what do I wait for?
My hope *is* in you."

MARK 12:43-44

So He called His disciples to *Himself*
and said to them,
"Assuredly, I say to you that this poor widow
has put in more
than all those who have given to the treasury;
for they all put in out of their abundance,
but she out of her poverty put in
all that she had,
her whole livelihood."

GOD'S POWER

Look at Deuteronomy 8:18: *And you shall remember the LORD your God, for it is He who gives you power to get wealth, that He may establish His covenant which He swore to your fathers, as it is this day.* The farmer may plow the field and sow the seed and sometime after that go to the fields to reap the harvest. But who does the work? How incredibly powerless is the farmer without God! See, without the forces of nature coming together to germinate and grow the seed, there would be no harvest.

Nothing we do can be done without the power of God. I am always amazed at how we continually forget, or just take for granted, the things God does for us. All of the things on this earth that His hands control never cease to amaze me. If we are going to assure ourselves of the greatness of the future God has intended for us in His plans, then part of our stewardship has to be the recognition of all that He gives us—the recognition that His hand is in everything we do. He alone gives us the ability to produce wealth. If we believe we are assuring our future on our own, we need to look around and realize all that we would not have if it were not for the awesome power of God.

DAY 8

JOSHUA 22:5
But take careful heed to do
the commandment
and the law which Moses the servant of the
LORD commanded you,
to love the LORD your God,
to walk in all His ways,
to keep His commandments,
to hold fast to Him,
and to serve Him with all your heart
and with all your soul.

DEUTERONOMY 6:4-5
"Hear, O Israel: The LORD our God,
the LORD *is* one!
You shall love the LORD your God
with all your heart,
with all your soul, and with all your strength."

MASTERS OF MONEY

Is it difficult to avoid the temptations of the world and not yield to what the majority seems to be doing? I remember Chuck Colson saying that the will of the majority is not necessarily the will of God. People who are lovers of money more than lovers of God will often yield to the temptations of the world. The Christian steward, however, is not mastered by money; the Christian steward masters money. The Bible clearly tells us that we cannot serve God and money. I do not believe this means money is a bad thing. I certainly do not believe prosperity is evil. God certainly wants us to prosper in all that we do. I know many people who have mastered their money for the Kingdom of God.

A good steward learns how to make money serve God. You may believe you are one of the greatest multitaskers ever to live, but trust me, 100 percent and all of your heart means just that—100 percent and all of your heart. There is no more to give to something else if you are truly giving 100 percent to the Lord. You see, God knows we will serve what is in our hearts. We each need to make sure our hearts are filled with the love, grace, mercy, and faithfulness of

God. A good and faithful master of his money learns how to make his money, his talents, all of his blessings, serve the One who has blessed him.

DAY 9

1 SAMUEL 2:30
Therefore the LORD God of Israel says:
"I said indeed *that* your house and the house
of your father
would walk before Me forever."
But now the LORD says:
"Far be it from Me; for those who
honor Me I will honor,
and those who despise Me shall
be lightly esteemed."

JOHN 5:23
That all should honor the Son
Just as they honor the Father.
He who does not honor the Son
does not honor the Father who sent Him.

Just Say "Yes!"

There are four attitudes we can take toward God's will for our life. We can say "no" to God; we can say "perhaps"; we can say "someday"; *or we can say "YES."* Although the first three answers may cause us some conflict, we can rest assured that when we say "Yes!" to God, all conflict will cease. Your work will take on a dignity and an honor you have never before realized as you become a partner with God in eternal enterprise. If you have not yet said "Yes!" to God in all things, you need to know it is an essential part of your stewardship.

If we want to know God's will for our lives, we need to be willing to say "Yes!" to all He gives us and be willing to say "Yes!" to His partnership in managing all He gives us. There cannot be any exceptions; there cannot be just a little piece of your life you have reserved for the world. You cannot straddle the fence. You cannot have one foot in the Kingdom of God and one foot in the world—even if it is your business world. It is a resounding "Yes!" that should be our attitude to God's will for our lives.

Day 10

1 Corinthians 15:56-58

The sting of death *is* sin, and the strength
of sin *is* the law.
But thanks *be* to God,
who gives us the victory through
our Lord Jesus Christ.
Therefore, my beloved brethren,
be steadfast, immovable,
always abounding in the work of the Lord,
knowing that your labor is not in vain
in the Lord.

John 12:26

If anyone serves Me, let him follow Me;
and where I am, there My servant will be also.
If anyone serves Me,
him *My* Father will honor.

LIKE IT OR NOT

I am amazed that we sometimes resent the mentioning of money and stewardship from the pulpit, yet it's repeatedly mentioned in the Bible. And I am *always* amazed at how many people insist that Jesus did not, in so many words, command or mandate that we tithe or give money. Yet nowhere in Scripture do we find Jesus ever lowering *any* of the standards set out in the Old Testament. He always raised them.

Do we really believe Jesus would have placed less value on the idea of tithing or giving back? First Corinthians 15 is an awesome affirmation of Christian hope and everlasting life. It is one of the basic passages in the New Testament. At the end of the passage, in the first verse of 1 Corinthians 16, Paul says, *Now concerning the collection for the saints...* You see, the collection was as sacred to Paul as all the other things in 1 Corinthians 15.

Like it or not, giving is the inevitable consequence of true Christian faith. I often talk on the radio and take opportunities when speaking to share this concern: that I hope the inability or lack of conviction to speak about giving from the pulpit will not leave an impres-

sion that giving to the Lord's work is just not
that important or necessary. This, I am afraid,
could have a devastating effect on Christendom.
How do you feel about messages from the
pulpit to give and tithe? Consider today what
Jesus had to say about giving to others to
advance the Kingdom.

DAY 11

2 CORINTHIANS 1:21-22
Now He who establishes us with you in Christ
and has anointed us *is* God,
who also has sealed us
and given us the Spirit in our hearts
as a guarantee.

EPHESIANS 1:14
Who is the guarantee of our inheritance
until the redemption
of the purchased possession, to the praise of
His glory.

MASTER'S MONEY

Look at Luke 19:12-13: *Therefore He said: "A certain nobleman went into a far country to receive for himself a kingdom and to return. So he called ten of his servants, delivered to them ten minas, and said to them, 'Do business till I come.'"* The servants, even the unfaithful servants, never referred to the money as their own, but always as "the master's property," saying, "*Your talents.*" Each of the servants freely acknowledged his master's ownership of the money.

They were much like us—stewards of the Master's money. We, too, have been entrusted as stewards, but think about *until the Master returns.* The Lord is going to return someday, or someday we will be facing Him. Will we have been good stewards? Faithful stewards or unfaithful? Will we have used His resources wisely? Maybe we will be so afraid of using it unwisely that we will do nothing with it.

I remember, as my wife and I struggled financially through so many difficult years, how hard it was to develop a habit of giving—to let it go. After all, we were letting go of that which we would have died to have some years ago. The temptation is to keep it all—above what should be set aside for that rainy day, for those troubled times—or to keep it all for a need that *might* arise. It is very tempting to love and desire to serve the Lord, yet perhaps, even while serving the Lord, to simultaneously be so fearful of using His provisions *unwisely* that we do nothing with them. Sadly, those provisions never bring any honor and glory to the Lord.

DAY 12

JEREMIAH 9:23-24
(NIV)

This is what the LORD says:
"Let not the wise man boast of his wisdom
or the strong man boast of his strength
or the rich man boast of his riches,
but let him who boasts boast about this:
that he understands and knows me,
that I am the LORD, who exercises kindness,
justice and righteousness on earth,
for in these I delight,"
declares the LORD.

GALATIANS 6:14

But God forbid that I should boast
except in the cross of our Lord Jesus Christ,
by whom the world has been crucified to me,
and I to the world.

ABILITY WITHOUT
OUR CREATOR

In 1 Corinthians 4:7, Paul writes, *For who makes you differ from another? And what do you have that you did not receive? Now if you did indeed receive it, why do you boast as if you had not received it?* I believe it's nothing less than pride and sinful ignoring of God's goodness and blessings that cause those who have created and accumulated wealth to boastfully say, "Look what I have achieved by my own ability and power."

The Bible is full of examples of human pride—and of human failure because of that pride. In 2 Chronicles alone, there are a number of examples of kings and great people who believed for a moment that all they had achieved was accomplished by their own power. We do not have to look further than the pages of the Bible to see how God dealt with them. They never got to enjoy the fruits of what God had given them. They missed God's plan. God was working hard with them, and through them, to assure greatness for their future; yet, they lost their ability to recognize the source of it all.

Let's thank God that we are not left to our

own ability and power. In our stewardship, we remember that all we have and all we are could not be without our Creator.

DAY 13

1 CORINTHIANS 1:8-9
Who will also confirm you to the end,
that you may be blameless
in the day of our Lord Jesus Christ.
God *is* faithful, by whom you were called
into the fellowship of His Son,
Jesus Christ our Lord.

1 JOHN 1:3
And truly our fellowship *is*
with the Father and
with His Son
Jesus Christ.

Cooperate with Him

Look at 1 Corinthians 7:23-24: *You were bought at a price; do not become slaves of men. Brethren, let each one remain with God in that state in which he was called.* I know that it is a bit of stretch, but if we were to look at that verse from a stewardship standpoint, it might mean, *Take God with you into your business.* It means to be in fellowship with Him, to be dependent upon Him, and to recognize He wants to be with us in all we do. Our future is dependent upon our work, our job, and a lot of things outside of church. So many Christians today have a specific, so-called Christian walk at work that is very different from their Christian walk on Sundays. Of course, they believe God would understand their behavior—that He would expect that they do whatever is necessary in their business world in order to succeed. But thinking this way is not part of God's plan or His intention for your future.

If you are going to fully cooperate with Him and strive to assure *His* great future for your life, then it will help you to understand that you are called to be a good steward of all He has given you. This means you are account-able for all of your business transactions as well as the transactions between you and your children, other relatives, and friends. Accountability is not limited to the transactions between you and your church or within your close small group of Christian friends. God wants you to cooperate with Him and to recognize Him in *all* of your life. Most importantly, abiding with God means to be in cooperation with Him because we are stewards of all that with which He has blessed us, including our business transactions and our work.

DAY 14

JEREMIAH 3:11-12
Then the LORD said to me,
"Backsliding Israel has shown herself
more righteous than treacherous Judah.
Go and proclaim these words
toward the north, and say:
'Return, backsliding Israel,' says the LORD;
'I will not cause My anger to fall on you.
For I *am* merciful,' says the LORD;
'I will not remain angry forever...'

MATTHEW 23:23
"Woe to you, scribes and Pharisees,
hypocrites!
For you pay tithe of mint and
anise and cummin,
and have neglected the weightier
matters of the law:
justice and mercy and faith.
These you ought to have done,
without leaving the others undone.

OUR DEBT

Romans 12:1 says, *I beseech you therefore, brethren, by the mercies of God, that you present your bodies a living sacrifice, holy, acceptable to God, which is your reasonable service.* Our "reasonable service" is an all-inclusive dedication of ourselves. It includes our affections, our energies, our minds, and our bodies. I think what Paul is asking sometimes seems rather extreme to some people. He is asking us—those who believe in the Lord—to offer *ourselves* as living sacrifices while we are here on earth. Have you ever really thought about what that might mean or what that might look like? It certainly could mean that, since our bodies are living sacrifices, we ought to take care of our physical well-being as well as our spiritual well-being. But to dedicate our whole selves to Him definitely means all the things I have already listed: our affections, our energies, our minds, our spirits and souls, our lives, our resources, our time, and maybe most importantly, our gratitude. Isn't offering our whole selves the only reasonable living sacrifice we can offer as partial payment of our debt to God? Our gifts of money are gifts of ourselves as we offer them in view of God's mercies toward us.

Paul certainly understood that the debt we owe our Lord is not anything we could ever begin to repay. We probably won't know the magnitude of the gift God has given us until we reach the gates of heaven. Since our debt can never be repaid because the Lord has already paid the entire penalty for our sins, let's give ourselves—our whole selves—as living sacrifices in gratitude for the debt He paid.

DAY 15

PSALM 29:11
The LORD will give strength
to His people;
The LORD will bless
His people
with peace.

ACTS 20:35
I have shown you in every way,
by laboring like this,
that you must support the weak.
And remember the words of the
Lord Jesus, that He said,
"It is more blessed to give than to receive."

PASS IT ON

I have written about responding to God as He would expect us to respond and that His blessings will pour out over us. God blesses us so that we might bless others. We need to be collaborators; we need to be partners and instruments of God here on earth. In Matthew 10:8, Jesus made an announcement to His disciples. He said, *Freely you have received, freely give.* We sometimes forget it's not always the blessings we have *received* that give us joy; it's the blessings we *give* that truly bless others. It is the gifts we pass on that can bring us the most joy. Isn't that what stewardship is?

Stewardship is being able to let go and give freely that which God has given us freely. Remember God has not given to us just because He loves us and wants to see us prosper, or because we have given Him glory, praise, and recognition for all we have. He truly does want us to pass it on. As He ensures a wonderful future for our lives, He wants us to spread that news and tell others—to give freely financially and of our time, resources, and talents, so that we might pass on His message. What a blessing we can be to others as we share and contribute our talents and resources.

Day 16

Proverbs 3:9-10
Honor the LORD with your possessions,
And with the firstfruits of all your increase;
So your barns will be filled with plenty,
And your vats will overflow with new wine.

1 Thessalonians 3:12
And may the Lord
make you increase and abound in love
to one another and to all,
just as we *do* to you,

HE OWNS IT ALL

"Bring all the tithes into the storehouse, That there may be food in My house, And try Me now in this," says the Lord of hosts, "If I will not open for you the windows of heaven and pour out for you such blessing that there will not be room enough to receive it." Malachi 3:10 clearly points out the blessings that come as a result of our tithing, but our stewardship comes before our tithe. All that we have is the Lord's. He owns it all. Malachi points out very specifically how the floodgates of God's blessings will open upon us. Talk about an incredible, exciting future for our lives, knowing that as we bring our offerings and glory to God, He assures us we will not even have room for the blessings that He will give us.

I think one of the things the Lord is saying through Malachi is that our hearts will even overflow with the blessings He will give us. Have we ever thought of tithing and giving as acts of worship? They are. These are awesome acts of worship. We have responsibility, however, as stewards for the administration of *all* of our income—not just our tithes and the money we have set aside for giving and bringing glory and honor to the Lord, but for all God has given us. Not just one tenth, but *all*. Remember—He owns it all.

DAY 17

MATTHEW 10:8
Heal the sick,
cleanse the lepers,
raise the dead,
cast out demons.
Freely you have received,
freely give.

JOHN 15:7-8
If you abide in Me,
and My words abide in you,
you will ask what you desire,
and it shall be done for you.
By this My Father is glorified,
that you bear much fruit;
so you will be My disciples.

ROBBING GOD

Look at Proverbs 11:24: *There is one who scatters, yet increases more; and there is one who withholds more than is right, but it leads to poverty.* I have seen many ways of using and misusing money, but the most frustrating is when money is not being used at all, when it is withheld from being used in God-honoring ways. What a thought—to be robbing God. Can you imagine hoarding, saving, and storing away all God has blessed you with and never having the opportunity to further the Kingdom of the gospel? Can you imagine never having the opportunity to gain even greater riches because we are keeping from God and God's work what is rightfully His?

I have seen people who believe they have a very strong obligation to provide for their families. They provide for themselves and their families tenfold—in excess—never allowing themselves to be used by God for His purposes. They give thanks to God for what they have received but do not give back to Him. Proverbs tells us that withholding and robbing God leads to poverty. If this is not referring to the experience of earthly poverty, I shudder to think of the poverty Proverbs *is* talking about.

If we expect our future to be bright because of God's hand in our life, then we need to be participating with Him in sharing what He has given us. As believers, we need to guard ourselves against the sin of robbing God, and to understand that, as servants, we are accountable to God. We should faithfully and freely be distributing our increases as the Lord continues to fill our storehouses.

DAY 18

MALACHI 3:7-8
Yet from the days of your fathers
You have gone away from My ordinances
And have not kept *them*.
Return to Me, and I will return to you,"
Says the LORD of hosts.

"But you said,
'In what way shall we return?'
"Will a man rob God? Yet you
have robbed Me!
But you say,
'In what way have we robbed You?'
In tithes and offerings."

ISAIAH 28:29
This also comes from the LORD of hosts
Who is wonderful in counsel
and excellent in guidance.

WHAT IS MINE?

I like the idea that tithing and giving should be an expression of our love for the Lord. They are expressions and examples of our walk as Christians. Certainly the blessings and possessions we accumulate are an expression of the Lord's blessing in *our* lives. As we think of tithing and giving as being an expression of our stewardship and our love for God, we must keep in mind that just because we tithe and continue to give from our increases does not mean we now have ownership over all that we did *not* give. It does not mean that because we have paid our one-tenth, or whatever we consider our tithe, that the balance of everything is now ours. We should not have a mentality of "what is mine is mine, and what is yours is yours." Remember the Lord owns it all.

Stewardship is not just giving a portion to God. It is our faithful administration and management of all God has given us. Tithing is an expression of our stewardship, and that stewardship should extend over all we have, not merely the percent that is our tithe. Think about how you are stewarding what's left over after you have given back to the Lord. Do you consider the remainder His? Remember the

Lord wants to be involved in the details of your life and can provide perfect guidance about using all His resources as you acknowledge they truly belong to Him.

DAY 19

1 CHRONICLES 29:9

Then the people rejoiced, for they had offered
willingly, because with a loyal heart they had
offered willingly to the LORD; and King David
also rejoiced greatly.

ZECHARIAH 1:3

Therefore say to them,
'Thus says the LORD of hosts:
"Return to Me," says the LORD of hosts,
"and I will return to you,"
says the LORD of hosts.'"

ACKNOWLEDGMENT TO GOD

Remember when David and the people brought their offerings to the Lord for the building of the temple as recorded in Chronicles? They gave as stewards. I love David's prayer as they presented those offerings to God. First Chronicles 29:11 says, *Yours, O Lord, is the greatness, The power and the glory, The victory and the majesty; For all that is in heaven and in earth is Yours; Yours is the kingdom, O Lord, And You are exalted as head over all.* What an awesome, definite acknowledgment of God's ownership of all we have!

David's attitude is an example of the attitude we are to possess when we give and attempt to be the best stewards we can be of God's resources. We are to acknowledge God and His greatness, His power, and His glory, as well as our own inability to do anything on our own. I know I have repeated this so many times, and I now continue to remind you that as you go through the day today, remember all that is around you is God's. Everything is the Master's. As you strive to live peacefully in your hearts, in unison with God, continue to acknowledge all He has done for you. Don't worry; He is not finished. He will continue to be faithful to you, blessing you, until your storehouses overflow, as long as you keep acknowledging *His* presence in your life.

DAY 20

2 CORINTHIANS 8:8
I speak not by commandment,
but I am testing the sincerity of your love
by the diligence of others.

HEBREWS 10:22
Let us draw near with a true heart
in full assurance of faith,
having our hearts sprinkled from
an evil conscience
and our bodies washed with pure water.

NO LEFTOVERS

God should be first in our giving, not last. Exodus 23:19 says, *The first of the firstfruits of your land you shall bring into the house of the LORD your God. You shall not boil a young goat in its mother's milk.* Wherever we receive our paychecks or income, we first need to recognize God's ownership of all we have received, immediately laying aside a portion for God. I remember many years ago when I started out in the insurance and financial planning business. I was not yet a believer, but I remember asking people to make a list of all their bills and expenses and to also make a list of all their income. I asked them to place their bills in order of importance in which they would pay them. Inevitably, the first priority was their mortgage payment, usually followed by their car payment. Because I wanted to make a case for contributing to their IRA or retirement plan, I would ask the question: "Where are you on this list? Do you realize out of all the income you have received and all the bills you have paid, nowhere on this list is there money set aside for you for your retirement planning." I used to tell them they ought to have themselves *first*, at the top of that list, and make sure they made their contribution to their IRA.

Oh, how I have changed! Of course, knowing what I know now, and having received the grace of God, I understand the first thing on that list ought to be God...not ourselves. Certainly, we have an obligation to pay our debts. But regardless of our financial income and circumstances, we must set aside a portion for God. A portion we set aside is as the Lord would lead—as our heart would lead (see Ps 31:3; Ex 25:2). Kingdom work should not just get whatever is left over at the end of the month or the end of the week. We are not to spend as we wish and give whatever is left over to God. God should be first in our giving, not last. This is the divine law of our giving. Giving to God first will continue to open doors to the joys and blessings of faithful stewardship.

Day 21

Deuteronomy 33:3
Yes, He loves the people;
All His saints *are* in Your hand;
They sit down at Your feet;
Everyone receives Your words.

1 Thessalonians 1:3
Remembering without ceasing
your work of faith, labor of love, and
patience of hope in our Lord Jesus Christ
in the sight of our God and Father.

FOR THE LOVE OF GOD

First Corinthians 13:3 says, *And though I bestow all my goods to feed the poor, and though I give my body to be burned, but have not love, it profits me nothing.* Our love of God and men must be the reason our gifts and giving flow. Giving that flows from our love of God is God's light. There is a passage in Galatians 5:22 that talks about the fruit of the Spirit. I am sure many of you are familiar with that verse. It says that the first fruit *is* love. It does not say the fruits *are* love, peace, patience, and so on. It does not use a plural, but a singular. You see, the fruit of the Spirit is love. All of the other fruits of the Spirit are built upon this foundation of love, just as the foundation of love is built upon the rock of Jesus Christ.

My youngest daughter once accused me of being judgmental about a boy she liked. I reminded her that I was not being judgmental at all; I was just being a "fruit inspector." One day the Lord will inspect our fruit. Will He find that love was a driving force in our giving?

God so loved the world that He gave His only begotten son. We always must be focused on giving because we love. Giving ought to be the result of the love we have for the Lord, an outgrowth of the stewardship we feel for the gospel and a desire to see the Kingdom of God grow. Loveless giving is lifeless giving. Our tithes and offerings should not be out of obligation or guilt, but our giving must flow freely because we share the love of God.

DAY 22

COLOSSIANS 3:23
And whatever you do, do it heartily,
as to the Lord and not to men.

EPHESIANS 3:19
To know the love of Christ which passes
knowledge;
that you may be filled with
all the fullness of God.

FAITHFUL GIVING

Look at 1 Corinthians 15:58: *Therefore, my beloved brethren, be steadfast, immovable, always abounding in the work of the Lord, knowing that your labor is not in vain in the Lord.* We are called as faithful servants to give ourselves fully to the Lord and His work. Do we know our stewardship, our giving, and our worship is to be as fully devoted followers of Christ? Do we trust that our labor is not in vain? Even if we do not recognize the fruits of our labor in our devotion to Christ here on earth, one of our goals has to be to hear these words from the Lord, *"Well done, good and faithful servant"* (Ma 25:21). Our labor, our work, our worship, and our following of Christ should not just be for our joy here on earth, though the Lord promises we will know that joy on earth. It should be out of our faithfulness to the Lord.

It is difficult, isn't it, to continue to work and give and strive for what seems to be in vain or sometimes useless in this world? But what a reward we will have for our labor as we continue to be devoted followers of Christ, faithful in our giving and our stewardship out of the love we share for God and for His Kingdom.

Our giving should never be out of guilt or obligation but should abound out of the love of God we share.

Day 23

Deuteronomy 25:13-15

"You shall not have in your bag differing
weights, a heavy and a light.
You shall not have in your house differing
measures, a large and a small.
You shall have a perfect and just weight,
a perfect and just measure,
that your days may be lengthened in the land
which the LORD your God is giving you."

Micah 6:11

Shall I count pure *those* with
the wicked scales,
And with the bag of deceitful weights?

GIVE AND GET

Look at Luke 6:38: *Give, and it will be given to you: good measure, pressed down, shaken together, and running over will be put into your bosom. For with the same measure that you use, it will be measured back to you.* Those are the words of Jesus. The measure you give will be the measure you get back. Think about the joy we can receive and prosperity of our future in God! I'm amazed by how many people do not take that verse to heart and how many Christians do not understand what it means. Sometimes we have one measure of giving in our personal lives that is very different than the measure we have of giving in our business lives. Sometimes we have a different measure of giving to our family, to the people we seem to care the most about here on earth, than we might for a ministry or even our church. Yet we expect God to have this remarkable equality in the way He gives back to us.

Well, as Jesus says in this passage, we will have equality in the measure He gives back to us. This passage is one we ought to remember as we think about giving and getting. Now Jesus obviously did not mean that if you were to give a hundred dollars to your church, the church would give you back a hundred dollars. He meant your spiritual blessings would be equal to your degree of stewardship. Jesus is just reminding us that our giving and our stewardship need to be a two-way street. Just as we certainly expect God's faithfulness to His promises, we are to be faithful to what He asks of us.

DAY 24

PSALM 119:14-16

I have rejoiced in the way of
Your testimonies,
As *much as* in all riches. I will meditate on
Your precepts,
And contemplate Your ways.
I will delight myself in Your statutes;
I will not forget Your word.

EPHESIANS 2:7

That in the ages to come
He might show the exceeding
riches of His grace
in *His* kindness toward us
in Christ Jesus.

TRUE RICHES

Remember the parable in Luke's Gospel of the unfaithful steward. Jesus says this, *"Whoever can be trusted with very little can also be trusted with much, and whoever is dishonest with very little will also be dishonest with much. So if you have not been trustworthy in handling worldly wealth, who will trust you with true riches?"* (Lk 16:10-11, NIV). I remember that when I first came to the Lord, I would pray for God's blessings upon my work and all that I had. At one point, I had to look back, wondering if I had been a good steward with the little things He gave me. Unfortunately, I realized that, "Why would He bless me with more when I had not been faithful in the little He had given me?"

Are you a good and faithful steward of the least of the things God has given you? Do you thank God for the routine and mundane things of your daily life? Are you a good steward over those little things or do you just take them for granted? If you want to enjoy true riches and you want to truly be blessed, knowing all that God has in store for you, you must first be able to enjoy, and be a good steward over, the least God has given you. One of the things Jesus is speaking about in this verse is being trusted with the little things, that we might enjoy true riches...the riches of His mercy, His forgiveness, and His peace. He wants us to enjoy all that He would like to bless us with—most importantly, the greater riches He has for us.

True riches are an increased capacity to enjoy, to serve, and to live abundantly. True riches can only be found through good, faithful and trustworthy stewardship over the little things as well as the larger things. Remember to give thanks today and to think about your stewardship over the everyday, mundane, little things with which the Lord has blessed you.

Day 25

Deuteronomy 1:30-33

The LORD your God, who goes before you,
He will fight for you,
according to all He did for you in Egypt
before your eyes,
and in the wilderness where you saw how the
LORD your God
carried you, as a man carries his son,
in all the way that you went until you
came to this place.'
Yet, for all that, you did not believe
the LORD your God,
who went in the way before you to search out a
place for you to pitch your tents, to show you
the way you should go,
in the fire by night and in the cloud by day.

Luke 12:13-15

Then one from the crowd said to Him,
"Teacher, tell my brother to divide the
inheritance with me."
But He said to him,
"Man, who made Me a judge or an
arbitrator over you?"
And He said to them, "Take heed and beware of
covetousness, for one's life does not consist in
the abundance of the things he possesses."

PARTNERSHIP

How would you feel if God came down, sat at your kitchen table, and said to you that He would like to be a partner with you in whatever it might be—perhaps a business venture or managing your daily income? Now how would you feel if you were told He has already done that? God tells us through Scripture that He wants to help us and to be with us. And we are promised that He is faithful to hold up His end of the partnership. If we like what God has done in our lives, yet we begin to grow and hoard our prosperity and just accumulate all He has given us, that is not a partnership. God would not want that for His half of the deal. Remember He is our partner. We want to be in unison with God for all of our decisions, just as we would be with our spouse.

Jesus tells the story of a man who pulled down his barns to build larger ones, and then the farmer said to himself that he had laid up much for many years, and he could take it easy. Now he would "eat, drink, and be merry." The Lord called him a fool because he thought he could put the real values of life in a barn. The farmer's difficulty was that he thought his life consisted of the abundance of things. The farmer forgot God's involvement in this partnership. He forgot God would not have wanted him to hoard his abundance but to give his increase or a portion of his increase to the things of God. The farmer decided to disregard his partner's wishes in the way he ran things.

In true Christian stewardship, we are partners and coworkers with God. We need to be conscious of what our partner would have us do with our resources and to understand that our partnership is also there to grow a true understanding of the real value of life.

DAY 26

EXODUS 15:12-13

You stretched out Your right hand;
The earth swallowed them.
You in Your mercy have led forth
The people whom You have redeemed;
You have guided *them* in Your strength
To Your holy habitation.

1 CHRONICLES 16:29-31

Give to the LORD the glory *due* His name;
Bring an offering, and come before Him.
Oh, worship the LORD in the beauty
of holiness!
Tremble before Him, all the earth.
The world also is firmly established,
It shall not be moved.
Let the heavens rejoice,
and let the earth be glad;
And let them say among the nations,
"The LORD reigns."

THE DEBT WE OWE

Doesn't it sometimes seem you will forever be in debt, whether it be financially or to your fellow man? It seems like it's never going to end. But I hope, as Christians, we recognize our debt to God. I am privileged and blessed now to enjoy some prosperity and to find joy in all with which the Lord has blessed me, but I remember all too well what it was like to know and feel the stress and anguish of incredible debt. I had been in dispute with a former partner of mine. I was not a believer at the time, and I spent seven years in federal court suing this former partner for the wrongdoing he had committed. I had incurred millions of dollars worth of debt. I remember a couple of years before the case finally completed, I accepted Jesus Christ as my Lord and Savior. The incredible bills and debt had grown to a point that I had nowhere to turn. We continued the court case and won.

I often tell people that I lost so many battles in those seven years that winning the war was hardly worth it. I was convicted to make good on all of my debt, although I was not legally obligated at that point. That was hard for me to swallow, but after seven years of anguish, paying everybody to whom I owed anything meant that my wife and I had practically nothing left. We were starting over again. But somehow, out of the grace of God, I was able to recognize His goodness in all of it and certainly had an opportunity to feel His love. I gained an understanding that we owe God for all He gave us and that debt can never be fully discharged. It is the one debt I was, still am, and always will be unable to repay.

Fortunately, I learned quickly that we are able to pay something on accounts. If we are faithful to God, and faithful stewards of His love and of the gifts and the talents He has given us as well as all the resources we have in our lives, we will continue to see and appreciate His faithfulness to us. Do you have something you can pay on your debt account to the Lord? See, our stewardship is just that. Every time we return and give back, we are making a small payment on our account.

DAY 27

ISAIAH 55:1-2

"Ho! Everyone who thirsts,
Come to the waters;
And you who have no money,
Come, buy and eat.
Yes, come, buy wine and milk
Without money and without price.
Why do you spend money for
what is not bread,
And your wages for *what* does not satisfy?
Listen carefully to Me, and eat *what is* good,
And let your soul delight itself in abundance."

2 CORINTHIANS 9:6-7

But this *I say*: He who sows sparingly
will also reap sparingly,
and he who sows bountifully
will also reap bountifully.
So let each one *give* as he purposes
in his heart,
not grudgingly or of necessity;
for God loves a cheerful giver.

HIS WILL BE DONE

"Your kingdom come. Your will be done on earth as it is in heaven" (Lk 11:2). What is the will of God for your life and my life? Sometimes I think we will never be able to answer this question completely—at least I won't: What is His will, His *total* will, for my life? But I do know the Bible speaks more often about stewardship than it does about salvation. We sometimes forget, as simple as it may seem that God knows the way His Kingdom will come is through faithful stewardship of the resources He gives His partners here on earth.

I know stewardship is so important to the Lord because it means the proclamation of the gospel. God's will for our lives is that His will be done—that we would be faithful stewards; that we would grow in prosperity so we might prosper the Kingdom of God. God's will is that we earn our money honestly, that we do not become wasteful, and that we use our resources wisely. Most of all, God's will is that we use our resources for His glory and that we give glory to Him for all the blessings He has given us.

DAY 28

DEUTERONOMY 8:17-18

Then you say in your heart,
'My power and the might of my hand have
gained me this wealth.'
"And you shall remember
the LORD your God,
for *it is* He who gives you power to get wealth,
that He may establish His covenant which He
swore to your fathers,
as *it is* this day."

1 TIMOTHY 6:17

Command those who are rich
in this present age
not to be haughty, nor to trust
in uncertain riches
but in the living God,
who gives us richly all things to enjoy.

MATTER OF TRUST

Do you know anybody who has said, "I will trust you with my immortal soul, but I won't trust you with my perishable, material possessions?" Have you ever wondered why Jesus warned about the perils of riches? He even urged the rich young ruler to dispose of his wealth because it had become his god. As believers, we recognize that this man was not lost or saved in proportion to his poverty or wealth. He was saved in spite of them. At the same time, we should recognize that a person of great means has a greater responsibility, in that his coming to Christ also includes his wealth.

I'm surprised by how often I meet new believers who are perhaps from very affluent families and who are wealthy themselves. These are people who may have just inherited riches, and they are certainly ready to trust the Lord with their lives, but they hesitate in trusting the Lord with their possessions and their wealth. It is amazing how I can sit back and see how God has orchestrated everything in their lives to get them to where they are today, but sometimes they only see how He has put them in the right place and the right situation to recognize His saving grace. Yet that recognition does not always include their possessions.

If you have made a commitment to give your life as a living sacrifice to the Lord, you go to that place with everything you own—all of your possessions, your children, your spouse—*everything* with which the Lord has blessed you is included.

DAY 29

HABAKKUK 2:4
But the just shall live by his faith.

PHILIPPIANS 1:27
Only let your conduct be worthy
of the gospel of Christ,
so that whether I come and see you
or am absent,
I may hear of your affairs, that you
stand fast in one spirit,
with one mind striving together for
the faith of the gospel,

THE BEST SERVICE

As stewards, we should always ask ourselves, "In what way can I best serve my Master with what He has given me and placed under my management?" That should be the question that governs all of our actions when it comes to being trustees of that with which we have been blessed. Malachi 3:8 asks, *Will a man rob God?* In 1 Corinthians 4:2, Paul writes, *Moreover it is required in stewards that one be found faithful.* We need to keep this question before us constantly: "In what way can I best serve my Master?" We have to remember that we need to serve the Lord in all areas of our lives—not just the things that are easy, not just the things we truly want to do, but even the difficult things. This includes the issues we may feel we are hiding from the Lord or those issues that pertain to us personally or to our family. All those things need to be given to the Lord, and through all of those, we need to serve our Master.

I tell people as I have opportunity to manage their finances or to work with them on their estates, that if I do not know all the details of their lives—particularly as it pertains to their finances—I cannot be expected to adequately manage their affairs. I need to know everything they are doing in order to develop the best strategy for their financial future. The Lord wants everything we are doing to serve Him. When we reach that place, His blessings upon our lives will be incredible.

Day 30

Psalm 111:2-3
The works of the LORD *are* great,
Studied by all who have pleasure in them.
His work is honorable and glorious,
And His righteousness endures forever.

Acts 4:24
So when they heard that,
they raised their voice to God with
one accord and said:
"Lord, You *are* God,
who made heaven and earth
and the sea, and all that is in them."

TRUE POSSESSOR

I know that even now as you read this, there are certain things you own or possess or work toward that you truly believe are yours. There are some things you believe you have created by your own sweat or tears. We all have this human tendency. You may believe there are portions of your prosperity that are yours, and you may not have given them over to God. There are also stresses and strains and debt you may not have given over to the Lord as well. God is the owner and the possessor of all the good things in our lives. But we should not just give over to Him the things we know are obviously blessings from the Lord. As a matter of fact, it is not those things that probably give us the most heartache. It is the things with which we are struggling that we hesitate to give over to the Lord. He wants all of it. He wants all of the good things. He wants all of our struggles. He wants us to totally rely upon Him and lean upon Him in all we do and all we have.

We must first and always recognize the great truth of God's ownership of all things. He alone is the absolute proprietor. Scripture consistently teaches this great truth of ownership. Genesis 14:22 says this: *But Abram said to the* king of Sodom, *"I have raised my hand to the Lord, God Most High, the Possessor of heaven and earth."* Do you recognize the great truth that God is the owner of all things? Have you given Him thanks for His blessings and entrusted Him with your struggles?

DAY 31

DEUTERONOMY 14:22
You shall truly tithe all the
increase of your grain
that the field produces year by year.

MATTHEW 23:23
"Woe to you, scribes and Pharisees,
hypocrites!
For you pay tithe of mint and anise
and cummin,
and have neglected the weightier
matters of the law:
justice and mercy and faith.
These you ought to have done,
without leaving the others undone.

Principle and Interest

I'm still surprised that so many people think if they tithe one-tenth, then they must have ownership of the other nine-tenths. Remember the parable of the three servants in Luke 19. When the master returned from the foreign land, he did not simply demand a small portion of the increase, but he held his servants accountable for both the principle and the interest. It is important that, as a starting point in our stewardship, we understand that every dollar belongs to God.

I know the story of a fellow who went to the pastor of his church. He was a man of great means and owned a very expensive sports car. He wanted to buy a matching, very expensive sports car for his wife, and he did not understand why his wife said it was not the right thing to do. His wife said it was not proper stewardship of the money. He went to the pastor of the church and said he did not understand her perspective since he was extremely generous with his giving and, in fact, gave more than a 10 percent tithe to the church. So, did that not entitle him to do as he wished with the rest of his money? He did not understand how it could possibly be wrong to buy a second sports car. Although this is probably *not* an example most of us can relate to, it is an illustration of someone who believes that since he is giving to Kingdom work, which is a wonderful thing, that the rest of the money is his to do with as he wants. The truth is that we still have stewardship responsibility for all that we have. God gave us every dollar. He didn't give us only 10 percent of what we earn and then expect us to give back to Him that 10 percent. He gave it all to us.

As we attempt to be good stewards, we need to realize that all of it—all the principal, all the interest, everything we earn or have, even if it was given to us and was not earned, is God's, so we have an incredible responsibility to do the right thing with all of it. Think today about how you understand your responsibility for the remaining nine-tenths of all you have.

DAY 32

1 CORINTHIANS 3:9-11

For we are God's fellow workers;
you are God's field, *you are* God's building.
According to the grace of God which was
given to me,
as a wise master builder I have laid
the foundation,
and another builds on it.
But let each one take heed how he
builds on it.
For no other foundation can anyone lay than
that which is laid,
which is Jesus Christ.

MARK 16:20

And they went out and preached everywhere,
the Lord working with *them* and
confirming the word
through the accompanying signs. Amen.

OUR PRODUCTION

Whenever you see a movie or television show, the credits always list a number of different producers. There are producers, assistant producers, music producers, and more, all of them contributing to the outcome of the production. But none of those would probably be possible if it were not for the executive producer. Generally, the executive producer is someone who may have had very little to do with the actual intricacies of the movie. He or she is, however, probably the individual who has put up the majority of the money. Without the executive producer, or the money, the movie would never have happened.

Sometimes we get confused as we travel through our lives; we begin to believe we are the executive producer of our lives. We believe we are actually orchestrating what our children are doing; what schools they are attending; our ability to earn a living; the job we have; the amount of money we make; and how we invest, spend, and save it. We need to remember, as we accumulate and acquire possessions and wealth and continue to have the ability to earn a living, that none of us can acquire anything without the help of our own personal executive producer—the One who makes everything in our lives happen. We need to remember what God said to the children of Israel through Moses in Deuteronomy 8:18: *"And you shall remember the Lord your God, for it is He who gives you power to get wealth..."* As we consider our stewardship and all God has given us, remember who gives us the ability to produce wealth.

DAY 33

PROVERBS 16:3
Commit your works to the LORD,
And your thoughts will be established.

COLOSSIANS 3:23-24
And whatever you do, do it heartily,
as to the Lord and not to men,
knowing that from the Lord
you will receive the reward of the inheritance;
for you serve the Lord Christ.

WORK FOR CHRIST

Look at 1 Corinthians 10:31: *Therefore, whether you eat or drink, or whatever you do, do all to the glory of God.* Whether we work as a homemaker, a salesperson, an accountant, or a carpenter, I believe life becomes very different when we do our work for Christ. I remember when I first accepted Jesus Christ as my Lord and Savior. I had just heard a wonderful testimony from a fellow by the name of Dr. Ben Carson, who is a pediatric neurosurgeon. Just after that, I heard a message on the radio from Charles Stanley, who seemed to be speaking directly to me. I felt I had no choice but to pull my car over and accept Jesus Christ as my Lord and Savior, knowing that at this point in my life, He was my only hope.

The circumstances prior to that, and leading up to that day, I will always remember as a pivotal point in my life. It was not, however, until about a year later that I came to the realization that it was not enough to just accept Jesus Christ as my Lord and Savior, but in doing that, I needed to give *my life* over to the Lord. This included all of my life, everything in it, including my work. It was at that point that I felt my life changing dramatically. Now here I am, many years after that day, and I still need to give my work and my life over to the Lord daily.

What a joy we take in our work when it is for Christ, regardless of what it is. All of the duties in our daily life should be done for the glory of God. Working for Christ is good stewardship of all the talents He's given us—stewardship for God's glory. Do you truly want your future to be brighter? Do you want to feel and experience God's blessing upon your life? Then make sure you give your work and your life over to the Lord daily.

Day 34

2 Peter 1:3-4

As His divine power has given to us all things
that *pertain* to life and godliness,
through the knowledge of Him who called us
by glory and virtue,
by which have been given to us exceedingly
great and precious promises,
that through these you may be partakers of
the divine nature,
having escaped the corruption *that is* in the
world through lust.

Daniel 6:4

So the governors and satraps sought to find
some charge against Daniel concerning the
kingdom; but they could find no charge
or fault, because he *was* faithful; nor was there
any error or fault found in him.

NOT CORRUPT

One thing that always disappoints me is that, no matter where I go, I meet people who believe that wealth comes from corrupt people. I am not sure whether this comes from jealousy or if people really do believe that when people are well off—that is, what the world may consider wealthy—that surely corruption must be in their lives.

This is simply not the case. I am blessed to know many wealthy people who have a full, complete understanding of the origin of their wealth. If it were not for people like that, the proclamation of the gospel would be hindered, and the growth of so many ministries would not happen.

While it is true that every dollar going to ministry is of great help, those who have an understanding of God's faithfulness—who happen to be wealthy—are pleasing to the Lord. He wants us all to be wealthy in whatever way we can handle or whatever way is best for us in our situation. Remember a man named Joseph, who came from Arimathea and offered his tomb to bury Jesus Christ. He was a disciple of our Lord and Savior and, by the way, a very wealthy man. His wealth was used by God for the fulfillment of the Scriptures.

DAY 35

MATTHEW 28:18-20

And Jesus came and spoke to them, saying,
"All authority has been given to Me
in heaven and on earth.
Go therefore and make disciples
of all the nations,
baptizing them in the name of
the Father and of the Son and
of the Holy Spirit,
teaching them to observe all things that I have
commanded you;
and lo, I am with you always, *even* to the end
of the age." Amen.

MARK 16:15

And He said to them,
"Go into all the world and preach the gospel
to every creature."

Rearranging Our Lives

I once heard a missionary talk about rearranging your life's activities in light of the Great Commission. I don't think he meant that we need to become missionaries, preachers, or pastors. He meant we need to determine that the rest of our lives are going to count for the stewardship of the gospel that has been committed to us. We need to devote ourselves to "stewardship living" in every part of our lives, whether this is the stewardship of our property, our gifts, our talents, our time, or our wealth. We need to rearrange our activities in light of the Great Commission. The Great Commission very clearly says that we are to go, therefore, and make disciples of all the nations.

Rearranging the activities of our lives means that the verse from Matthew 28:19 is first and foremost in our minds and hearts—that all of the things we do, including working and spending our time and money, is in light of that Great Commission. I become more and more convinced every day that one of the greatest mission fields in the entire world is here in America—in your neighborhood, in your town. Unfortunately, that mission field is growing larger and larger every year. What are you doing to further the Kingdom of God?

DAY 36

MATTHEW 14:16-20
But Jesus said to them,
"They do not need to go away. You give them
something to eat."
And they said to Him,
"We have here only five loaves and two fish."
He said, "Bring them here to Me."
Then He commanded the multitudes to sit
down on the grass.
And He took the five loaves and the two fish,
and looking up to heaven,
He blessed and broke and gave the loaves to
the disciples;
and the disciples gave to the multitudes.
So they all ate and were filled,
and they took up twelve baskets full of the
fragments that remained.

MATTHEW 15:33
Then His disciples said to Him, "Where
could we get enough bread in the wilderness
to fill such a great multitude?"

THE GREAT MULTIPLIER

Our giving becomes an incredible power in the hands of Christ. With a few loaves and fishes, He can feed thousands. Some have said that because of the great things the Lord Jesus can do with small amounts, we don't need to give much. Maybe all we can give is a little, or a small amount, but we ought to give all we can and allow God, the Great Multiplier, to multiply our gifts tenfold for the good of the Kingdom. How much greater is tenfold when we give a great deal as we are able to do so?

I still sit back and think about the very lean years my wife and I experienced, and I wonder, "How did we ever put food on the table or pay bills?" Yet the Great Multiplier managed to make sure that somehow we had enough to do what was necessary. I still, to this day, wonder how it happened—it went so unnoticed sometimes. We should remember that Jesus fed the five thousand with not just a few loaves and fishes; He was given *all* the boy had. The multiplying power of Christ should encourage the one who can't give much to give a little, but it also should inspire those who can give abundantly more, to allow Christ to work an even mightier deed.

DAY 37

PROVERBS 11:25

The generous soul will be made rich,
And he who waters will also be
watered himself.

1 CORINTHIANS 1:9

God is faithful, by whom you were called
into the fellowship of His Son,
Jesus Christ our Lord.

FIRST THINGS FIRST

Have you ever wondered why so many people seem to come to the Lord during a crisis situation? I know my crisis situation certainly brought me to my knees—to help bring me to the Lord. I remember once flying from Atlanta to South Carolina, and next to me on this very short flight was a woman going to visit a teenage daughter, who had been in crisis just five months earlier. This mother spoke with great enthusiasm and pride about the incredible battle that was fought and won by her daughter. She went on to explain that she was, herself, a recovering alcoholic and had been sober for a year. I remember hearing and seeing the incredible joy on her face and in her eyes as she spoke of fighting a battle, and seeing her daughter fight a similar battle, and winning—finally beginning to get her life in order. She was a complete stranger to me, but I felt so excited and proud for her, for what God had done in her life.

I think sometimes our stewardship is like that. It is a battle that we need to fight continuously, to fight the battle against the world and what the world is calling us to do with our talents and resources, versus what the Lord may be calling us to do. One of my favorite verses in Scripture is 2 Timothy 4:7. Paul sums up thirty-some years of an incredible ministry in one verse. *I have fought the good fight, I have finished the race, I have kept the faith.* When Paul says he has kept the faith, he is drawing for us an image of his stewardship of Christian truth and of the gospel. Before we are able to be good stewards of the financial resources with which the Lord has blessed us, we must first be a good steward and a keeper of the faith the Lord has entrusted to us.

One of the first things we need to prioritize is the willingness to fight the battle ahead of us and the great joy we will take in staying focused and strong with perseverance and persistence as we keep the faith.

DAY 38

I CORINTHIANS 10:13

No temptation has overtaken you
except such as is common to man;
but God *is* faithful,
who will not allow you to be tempted beyond
what you are able,
but with the temptation will also make the
way of escape,
that you may be able to bear *it*.

I THESSALONIANS 5:23-24

Now may the God of peace Himself sanctify
you completely;
and may your whole spirit, soul, and body be
preserved blameless
at the coming of our Lord Jesus Christ.
He who calls you *is* faithful,
who also will do *it*.

PROCRASTINATION

You can almost hear the frustration in Joshua's voice: *"How long will you neglect to go and possess the land which the Lord God of your fathers has given you?"* (Jos 18:3). Oftentimes, we put off the larger jobs—the difficult, boring, or disagreeable ones—that lie before us. Procrastinating shows a lack of discipline or poor stewardship of one's time. In some cases, this can even show disobedience toward God. Stewardship of our time in jobs that we don't enjoy sometimes requires a certain amount of concentration, sometimes twice as much time, and lots of encouragement and accountability. Don't be tempted to procrastinate. Let's be good stewards of the time God gave us.

The Lord gave the Hebrews the land, and Joshua's faith—and desire to be obedient to God—probably created the frustration in him. Sometimes God gives us so many things, yet we neglect to take possession of them. Maybe it is just easier to keep asking, all the while procrastinating and taking what God has given us. Instead of giving in to procrastination, ask God to guide you in the stewardship of your time today.

DAY 39

MATTHEW 18:4
Therefore whoever humbles himself
as this little child
is the greatest in the kingdom of heaven.

2 KINGS 1:13
Again, he sent a third captain of fifty
with his fifty men.
And the third captain of fifty went up,
and came and fell on his knees
before Elijah, and pleaded with him,
and said to him:
"Man of God, please let my life and
the life of these fifty servants
of yours be precious in your sight."

HUMBLE HEART

In 2 Kings 1:13, there is a captain who comes to Elijah and pleads with him. He is different from the two captains who came before him in that his heart truly is humbled by being in front of such a man of God. I have often had the opportunity to meet people who have great resources, but one of the things that sets them apart from other worldly people with great resources is their humble regard for God, especially their attitude toward God and what He has done in their lives. God must be so pleased for a servant of His to have such an incredibly humble heart. This is the kind of heart we need to possess if we expect God's faithfulness to us.

How many times have we heard that our hearts have to be right before the Lord? Humility is one way our hearts need to be right. If we are going to be faithful stewards and servants of God, it will be shown or characterized by our humility and our attitude toward God and all that He has given us.

Day 40

Ephesians 1:18
The eyes of your understanding
being enlightened;
that you may know what is the hope
of His calling,
what are the riches of the glory of
His inheritance in the saints.

1 Kings 2:3
And keep the charge of the LORD your God:
to walk in His ways, to keep His statutes,
His commandments,
His judgments, and His testimonies,
as it is written in the Law of Moses,
that you may prosper in all that you do
and wherever you turn.

CONSUMED FOR
THE KINGDOM

In Scripture, we continually see God's warning about storing up. In Proverbs 23:4-5, we again are cautioned: *Do not overwork to be rich; Because of your own understanding, cease! Will you set your eyes on that which is not? For riches certainly make themselves wings; They fly away like an eagle toward heaven.* These verses certainly do not tell us to avoid being industrious, but as we are blessed with the ability to earn money, we need to have wise restraint rather than being consumed for the sake of money.

I am sure most of you have seen your money grow wings. I know I have. In raising children and putting them through college, I sometimes think I have actually *seen* wings on my money. It does seem as though it flies away as I sit back and wonder where it went. I am sure all of us can relate to those experiences. Though we are told not to be meaninglessly "storing up," we are certainly not called to be wasteful and frivolous in our spending habits. We need to have wise restraint, both in spending our money as well as when we are working for our money.

It all boils down to keeping the right heart,

to working for the sake of the Kingdom, to being consumed for the Kingdom of God. The Lord will bless us, and He will provide; as long as we are not sitting idly by, we can be assured He will bless us with all we need.

CONCLUSION

When we recognize the moving of God's complete and perfect hand in our lives, we begin to see His blessings in our daily walks. Our relationship with our Lord and Savior will be taken to a whole different level of fellowship, one in which He provides us with a deep sense of joy from serving Him. My prayer is that you will use these devotionals to start building a solid foundation on the understanding of the ownership of all with which the Lord has blessed you.

We should consider the things that we need to put in order. I believe that if we are going to be good stewards of all the Lord has given us—if we are going to grow closer to the Lord and advance the gospel of Jesus Christ through our stewardship—then we ought to be planning and ensuring that our good stewardship continued as well. The Bible encourages us to do things in an orderly way, so our life should be planned in an orderly way that will lead to good stewardship.

The Lord wants us also to be careful in our stewardship. He wants us to be responsible in our giving and our planning. As part of our stewardship, we need to understand that we do have to provide for our own care as we age, as well as for the care of those around us. Our ministry and our mission for the Lord will change as we age. I do not believe we are called to sit around and do nothing in our retirement age; we need to provide and make sure that we are good stewards over all of the money that He has given us for our own use as well as that which we have given to Kingdom work. In reference to the Levites, the Lord told Moses: *And at the age of fifty years, they must cease performing this work, and shall work no more* (Nu 8:25), but He goes on to mention that they are to continue to minister after their work is finished. If we work for the Lord in our stewardship and in the gifts that we give today, and we constantly and continually think about the stewardship of the gospel of Jesus Christ, then we need to consider *not* "Do I retire?" but rather "Into what form of service do I retire?"

As we contemplate our continued faithfulness to stewardship, we also need to focus on all the good that God has given us. We too often get caught up in what we do *not* have, just as the people of Israel as they grumbled in the desert (Nu 11). Amazing how quickly they forgot the harshness of Egyptian slavery. Their focus shifted from what God had given them in the form of manna—and freedom—to all that they did not have. For us to be effective stewards, our focus needs to be on the gifts that God has already given us.

Are we using those gifts properly? Are we serving God's purpose for us here on Earth? Are we waiting on the Lord's leading in our stewardship? The apostles were told to go out but also to wait for the power that they would receive from the Holy Spirit. Just because your heart is not convinced today about what you ought to be doing with your financial resources does not mean you should consider your stewardship unimportant.

Wait. God will do a great work with what He has given you if you are open to receiving His leading about your stewardship. Remember Ephesians 1:11-12, and ask God how He has chosen you according to His plan for us and for His purposes. Verse 12 points out that we who first trusted in Christ should be *to the praise of His glory*. I know that God's purposes are very different for each person, but ultimately God wants us to be obedient to His call on our lives and His purpose for us, that we might move forward with our lives, praising Him and glorifying Him in all that we do. If we can stay focused on achieving and accomplishing His purposes with the gifts, and the talents, and the resources that God has provided to us, then our closeness to God—our relationship with our Savior Jesus Christ—can only grow, and our stewardship can only be pleasing to Him.

As I travel about and speak to so many people, I am more convinced than ever that our personal relationship with Jesus Christ grows stronger every day that we make attempts to be good and faithful stewards of all that He has blessed us with. 1 Peter 1:15 says: *But as He who called you is holy, you also be holy in your conduct.* In all that we do, we are called to be holy. We are to be in the presence of God, to draw closer to God, to be holy in all that we do, in all that we are, and with all that He has blessed us, including our time, our health, our financial resources, and our talents. The heart of our stewardship should be being holy in all that we do.

A great verse to remember is 1 Thessalonians 5:17, which simply says, *Pray without ceasing.* As we are called to pray without ceasing, did you ever think that we were created by God so that we would also worship without ceasing? Being constantly mindful of faithful and good stewardship is an incredible act of worship. If part of your worship is to give even one dollar, one day's service, or your complete recognition of His blessings in your life then, with the Lord, I thank you for your faithful stewardship.

Psalm 101:6

My eyes shall be on the faithful of the land,
That they may dwell with me:
He who walks in a perfect way,
He shall serve me.

NOTES

NOTES